Lee Bailey's small bouquets

Clarkson Potter/Publishers

New York

Lee Bailey's small bouquets

a gift for all seasons

Text and Photographs by Lee Bailey

Published by Clarkson N. Potter, Inc., 201 East 50th Street, New York, New York 10022 and distributed by Crown Publishers, Inc. Member of the Crown Publishing Group.

CLARKSON N. POTTER, POTTER and colophon are trademarks of Clarkson N. Potter, Inc.

Manufactured in Japan

Design by Jim Christie

Library of Congress Cataloging-in-Publication Data
Bailey, Lee.
  Small bouquets / text and photographs by Lee
  Bailey—1st ed.
      p.   cm.
  1. Flower arrangement—Pictorial works.
I. Title. II. Title:
Small bouquets.   90-7411
  SB449.B24 1990   CIP
745.92′2—dc20
ISBN 0-517-57571-X
10 9 8 7 6 5 4 3 2 1
First Edition

Dedication
For Geraldine, Lizzie, two Elaines, Nora, Ruthie, Judy, Holland, Sherrye, Miss K., D.D., Mildred, Fern, and Amy—in no particular order.

Acknowledgments
Flowers from Teresa and Tony Babinski, Bayberry Nursery, Son Jardin, Betsy and Michael Yastremski, Billy Jarecki, and Tom Pritchard.

Containers from D. Heubner, D. Luck, F. Klotz, R. Mitchell, Pine Street Antiques, Fiocca, Tampopo, J. Robbins, D. Brooks, and J. Blum.

contents

A book on small flower bouquets will probably start vicious rumors that I am a hopeless romantic. To rebut such irresponsible speculation, I want to say right now that this book is — at least in part — the result of an astigmatism. To start with, I've always been pretty up-front with the fact that I am a flower nut, so it should come as no surprise that I've spent many contented moments staring at flowers. You know, simply standing there staring, hoping no one is watching

introduction and wondering what in the world I'm up to. But more than that, I've always been fond of seeing flowers — especially small ones — close up. For years this presented no problem. Then things started to get fuzzy around the edges, and I took to squinting a lot, most often when I tried to focus on something like violets while I was standing. Squinting worked for a time, but finally I would have to get down on one knee to see really clearly. That was actually okay, too. It was just the getting up after being on one knee for more than a few minutes that I didn't love. **So I got** into the habit of picking a few perfect specimens of whatever caught my fancy and putting them eye level, say in a glass of water on a windowsill in the kitchen, where I could give them an approving glance now and again. Alas, you know how we addicts are. After a while, a few stopped being able to do the trick; I needed a handful, enough to make a small bouquet. Well, you don't have to be any sort of mental giant to guess the rest. During spring, summer, and fall you never know where in my house you will come across these little bunches of flowers. **I don't know,** maybe

this does make me a nearsighted romantic. There are worse things. I could have had 20/20 vision. And look what a pleasure my astigmatism has been for me. **Anyway, here is** a little gift of flowers from me to you. **Lee Bailey, Bridgehampton, Long Island**

signs of

spring

Sure Signs

Daffodils and narcissus. Everywhere.

Splashed across the landscape.

Bright-faced Signs Pansies and
Johnny-jump-ups. Did you know *pansy*
means "thought"?

Astonishingly Fragrant Signs

Wood hyacinths.

Romantic Signs Lilies of the valley

represent the return of happiness.

And Cool Signs White violets represent

welcome.

good signs Tulips: a sensation

and a scandal when they hit

Vienna

from Con-

stantin-

ople. That

was about

1550. Next

there was

Holland and tulipomania. Still a

sensation today, I'd say.

some

roses

Some wild pink roses last hardly
a day.

Some old favorite roses bloom

almost all summer.

some

miniature

roses

are

almost

green

Some people used to believe that red roses were red because they had been stained by the blood of Venus,

Then some people associate white roses with purity. But did you know the white rose is also the symbol of silence? And all this time I thought silence was golden.

Stately Queen Elizabeth roses are here attended by modest Fairy roses.

Years ago almost all miniature roses
were referred to as ''Tom Thumb'' roses.

A perfect duet of colors — shades of
pink and old ivory roses.

Some yellow roses, among them Arlene Francis, Oregon, and Golden Masterpiece.

deep

Summer is too short
for me.
Summer is too hot
but not for me.
Summer means annuals
to me.
Here are bunches of
summer flowers
from me.

a few

flowers

A few flowers

are all you need

to make

a bouquet.

m i x   p o p p y   c o l o r s . . .

or

let

one

color

say

it

all

Mix together every pink flower you can find in your garden.

Mix small flowers with one big aster.

Mix all shades of pink dianthus with
small fern fronds.

Mix pansies and forget-me-nots.

Mix shades of daylilies.

Mix yellow and brown coreopsis and
accent with bright pink.

A few flowers are all you need to make

a bouquet.

and then

From the full heat of summer to the chill of autumn, sunflowers like it all. In shades from almost white to almost brown— stopping at yellow, gold, and orange along the way.

Italian sunflowers

Mexican sunflowers

a s

t h e

d a y s

d w i n d l e

d o w n

Tuberoses, sneezeweed, and more
Italian sunflowers

one

step

from

winter

Mixed fall sunflowers

can

spring

be

far

behind?